salsas & dips

salsas & dips

hamlyn

NOTES

The FDA advises that eggs should not be consumed raw. This book contains some dishes made with raw or lightly cooked eggs. It is prudent for more vulnerable people such as pregnant and nursing mothers, invalids, the elderly, babies and young children to avoid uncooked or lightly cooked dishes made with eggs.

Meat and poultry should be cooked thoroughly. To test if poultry is cooked, pierce the flesh through the thickest part with a skewer or fork—the juices should run clear, never pink or red. Keep refrigerated until ready for cooking.

This book includes dishes made with nuts and nut derivatives. It is advisable for those with known allergic reactions to nuts and nut derivatives and those who may be potentially vulnerable to these allergies, such as pregnant and nursing mothers, invalids, the elderly, babies and children, to avoid dishes made with nuts and nut oils. It is also prudent to check the labels of ingredients for the possible inclusion of nut derivatives.

First published in Great Britain in 2003 by
Hamlyn, a division of Octopus Publishing Group Ltd
2–4 Heron Quays, London E14 4JP

Copyright © Octopus Publishing Group Ltd 2003

ISBN 0 600 60895 6

A CIP catalogue record for this book is available from the British Library

Printed and bound in China

10 9 8 7 6 5 4 3 2 1

contents

introduction

Salsas and dips are popularly served with tortilla chips, potato chips, or vegetable sticks and served as finger food at parties, as "nibbles" with pre-dinner drinks or as a meal appetizer. However, the versatility of salsas and dips means their use extends way beyond "chips 'n' dips." A spoonful or two of either is just as likely to be served in a bun on a burger, as a topping for crostini, as a filling for baked potatoes, or as an accompaniment to salad or broiled, roasted or barbecued meat, poultry and fish.

Salsas

The word "salsa" means "sauce" in Spanish, but is now widely used to describe a type of relish comprising a colorful mixture of finely diced vegetables and/or fruit and seasonings—in effect a crunchy "salad." Salsas are usually made with uncooked ingredients, less common are salsas that are cooked and puréed. Mexican in origin and often spicy, salsas can range from mild to fiery hot. Nowadays, salsas are popular almost everywhere and the scope for suitable salsa ingredients has widened dramatically from the ripe tomatoes—or tomatillos for green salsa (*salsa verde*)—onion, garlic, chilies, and cilantro of a traditional Mexican salsa.

Virtually anything goes, so be inspired by the recipes on pages 10–27 and feel free to experiment. Try combining different fruits and vegetables with onions and/or garlic and chilies and/or peppers, together with sweet (fruit juice, honey, or sugar) and sour (lime juice, lemon juice, or vinegar) flavors plus salt and black pepper. Optional extras could include olive oil, finely grated fresh ginger, chopped olives, mustard seeds, and chopped fresh herbs such as cilantro, mint, sage, or parsley.

Uses for salsa

Although salsas are available bottled, or fresh from the deli counter, you cannot beat the taste of a homemade salsa. Aside from their popular partnership with tortilla chips, salsas are ideal for adding depth and flavor to a meal.

Being colorful, salsas make effective garnishes, while their raw crunchiness adds texture to soup or a grilled cheese sandwich. As a relish on the side, mild salsas are refreshing with a hot curry, while spicier versions make a tasty accompaniment to plainly cooked meats and fish like steamed salmon or chicken. Just as traditional fruit sauces are served with roasted pork, ham, and duck to cut their richness, fruity salsas with their zingy citrus/vinegar content can perform the same function. Tomato-based salsas make good bases for pizza toppings and pasta sauces and work well with scrambled or poached eggs. A fruity salsa made without onions makes a refreshing dessert.

Making salsa:

Salsas are simple to make and require just a sharp knife for fine dicing. Alternatively, you can use a food processor, but do make use of the pulse button so that the ingredients retain some texture instead of being pulverized. You can even buy a manually operated, purpose-made salsa maker, whose hand-cranked blade chops salsa ingredients to perfection.

The fruits and vegetables in salsas are usually used fresh although sun-dried or canned tomatoes, dried chilies, canned corn, and canned pineapple can all be used in a salsa. In addition, some ingredients benefit from light cooking before use to intensify their flavor—roasted peppers and broiled corn are good examples.

Dips

Whereas the origins of salsa lie in Mexican and Southwestern cooking, dips originate all over the globe, as the recipes on pages 28–47 demonstrate. From Mexico to Europe, the Middle East and Far East, every cuisine has its favorite dip and "dipper"—think of guacamole and tortilla chips, aïoli and French bread, hummus or baba ganoush and pita bread, raita and poppadums, peanut sauce and chicken skewers.

Dips make entertaining easy—most can be made in advance—and they are always popular with guests. Simply present people with a choice of dips, dippers and a napkin and let them help themselves. Use any leftover dip in sandwiches or baked potatoes, or as the basis for a sauce for pasta, rice, or noodles.

Shortcut dippers

There are plenty of suggestions for homemade accompaniments for dips on pages 48–63—from straightforward oven fries to the more involved vegetable tempura and beef satays for a special occasion. If time is short, however, store-bought standbys include breadsticks (available in mini lengths), tortillas, potato chips (scoop-shaped or ridged ones are perfect for dipping), corn chips, cheese straws, vegetable chips, rice cakes, pretzels, mini pita breads, or any of the appealing speciality breads now widely available.

Vegetable crudités are another quick option. Many supermarkets offer a selection of baby vegetables, such as baby carrots, which are just the right size for dipping. Sugar snap peas, cherry tomatoes, and button mushrooms are also ideal sizes, while vegetables such as celery, bell peppers, cucumber and zucchini need to be cut to length and cauliflower and broccoli need to be broken into florets. Again, to save time, many of these can be bought ready-to-eat.

Healthy options

Happily, salsas are low in fat and low in calories, if you need to be vigilant about what you eat. They are also packed with vitamins and are rich in fiber, making them a healthy option. You need to be a little more careful when choosing a dip—and of course what you use to dip into it! Many dips are based on cream, mayonnaise, or cream cheese. Some recipes can be adapted to use low-fat ingredients like cottage cheese and plain yogurt—raita is a good example—but can suffer from a loss of flavor as a result. However, low-fat mayonnaise, light cream cheese, and low-fat crème fraîche can often be substituted for the real thing and are a good compromise with regard to flavor and fat content. Vegetable crudités, pita bread, pretzels, and breadsticks are healthier accompaniments than chips and cheesy crackers.

1 small **red onion**, finely chopped

14 ounces small **vine-ripened tomatoes**, halved, seeded, and chopped

2 **garlic cloves**, crushed

$1/4$ cup **cilantro leaves**, chopped

salt and **pepper**

cilantro and tomato salsa

1 Put the red onion, tomatoes, garlic and cilantro leaves in a bowl and mix together. Season lightly with salt and pepper, then cover and chill for at least 30 minutes for the flavors to develop.

2 Serve with cold cuts or as a side dish with curries and other spicy foods.

Makes 1$^1/_2$ cups

Preparation time: 10 minutes, plus chilling time

3–4 tablespoons **lime juice**

2 tablespoons **olive oil**

a few drops of **Tabasco™
sauce**

1 small **garlic clove**, finely
chopped

$^1/_2$ small **red onion**, finely
chopped

2 large firm, ripe **tomatoes**,
skinned, seeded, and finely
chopped

2 large firm, ripe **avocados**,
halved, pitted, peeled, and
chopped

3 tablespoons finely chopped
cilantro leaves

salt and **pepper**

avocado and tomato salsa

1 Put the lime juice, olive oil,
Tabasco™, and garlic in a bowl and
whisk well to combine. Stir in the
onion, add the chopped tomato
and avocado and toss gently in the
dressing along with the chopped
cilantro. Season to taste with salt
and pepper.

Makes 1³/₄ cups

Preparation time: 10 minutes

TIP
A ripe avocado gives slightly when
you press it at the pointed end.
However, if you have an unripe
avocado and need to speed up the
ripening process, put it in a paper
bag with an apple or a banana.
The gases they give off help
accelerate ripening.

black bean, tomato and cilantro salsa

1 Drain the black beans and cook in a saucepan of salted boiling water for 45 minutes or according to the package instructions. Cool under cold running water and drain thoroughly.

2 Put the black beans in a bowl and add the chopped tomatoes, red and green chilies, garlic, lime zest and juice, olive oil, and cilantro leaves. Season generously with salt and pepper, then cover and leave to rest for 30 minutes before serving for the flavors to infuse.

Makes 1³/₄ cups

Preparation time: 15 minutes, plus resting time

Cooking time: 45 minutes

FOOD FACT
The black bean is also known as the turtle, Mexican or Spanish black bean, and black kidney bean. It is widely used in Latin American cooking and in recipes from the Southwest. It has a white inside and a mild flavor and should not be confused with the Asian or Chinese black bean, a type of soy bean that is salted and used as a flavoring.

³/₄ cup **black beans**, soaked for 8 hours or overnight

5 **plum tomatoes**, skinned and chopped

1 large **red chili**, seeded and finely chopped

1 large **green chili**, seeded and finely chopped

2 **garlic cloves**, finely chopped

grated zest and juice of 1 **lime**

3 tablespoons **olive oil**

¹/₄ cup chopped **cilantro leaves**

salt and **pepper**

5 **tomatillos**

2 **jalapeño chilies**, seeded and finely chopped

2 **garlic cloves**, finely chopped

$^1/_2$ **red onion**, finely chopped

3 tablespoons chopped **basil**

2 tablespoons **clear honey**

2 tablespoons **olive oil**

salt and **pepper**

green tomatillo salsa

Despite their name, tomatillos, which come from Mexico, belong to the same family as physalis and Chinese lanterns and not the tomato family. If you are pressed for time you can blend all the ingredients for this salsa in a food processor; this means that the finished result may be slightly slushy, but it will still taste fantastic.

1 Remove the outer leaves from the tomatillos and wash them thoroughly to remove any stickiness from the skins. Chop them finely and put them in a bowl with the chilies, garlic, onion, basil, honey, and olive oil. Mix well and season generously with salt and pepper. Serve immediately.

Makes 1$^3/_4$ cups

Preparation time: 15 minutes

1 small **red onion**, finely chopped

1 **garlic clove**, finely chopped

1 pound sweet ripe **tomatoes**, skinned, seeded, and chopped

1–2 sweet, moderately hot **red chilies**, seeded and finely chopped

$^1/_4$ cup finely chopped **cilantro leaves**

2 tablespoons finely chopped **parsley**

2 tablespoons **lime juice**

$^1/_4$ cup **olive oil**

pinch of **sugar**

salt and **pepper**

hot tomato salsa

This is a very useful basic tomato salsa. For variety, you can add chopped fresh herbs, such as mint, fennel, lovage, oregano, marjoram, dill, and tarragon. For a more gentle salsa, leave out the chili.

1 Put the onion, garlic, tomatoes, and chilies into a bowl. Add the cilantro and parsley and stir in the lime juice and olive oil. Season with a pinch of sugar and salt and pepper and mix lightly.

2 Cover and chill for 30–60 minutes, to let the flavors develop before serving.

Makes 1²/₃ cups

Preparation time: 10–15 minutes, plus chilling time

cucumber salsa

1 Halve the cucumber lengthwise and scoop out the seeds. Finely chop the cucumber and toss in a bowl with the cilantro, scallions, lemon or lime juice, sugar, and a little salt and pepper. Cover and chill for at least 30 minutes for the flavors to develop.

2 Serve with cold cuts or burgers and a mixed salad.

Makes 1¹/₄ cups

Preparation time: 10 minutes, plus chilling time

¹/₂ small **cucumber**

3 tablespoons chopped **cilantro leaves**

2 **scallions**, finely chopped

2 tablespoons **lemon** or **lime juice**

1 teaspoon **superfine sugar**

salt and **pepper**

2 **corn cobs**, stripped of husks and threads

$^1/_4$ cup **olive oil**

2 tablespoons **red onion**, finely chopped

4–6 tablespoons **lime juice**

2 dashes of **jalapeño sauce**

1 small **red chili**, seeded and finely chopped

$^1/_4$ small **red bell pepper**, cored, seeded, and finely chopped

1 large firm, **red plum tomato**, skinned, seeded, and finely chopped

$^1/_4$ teaspoon **ground coriander**

3 tablespoons finely chopped **cilantro**

1 firm, ripe **avocado**, halved, pitted, peeled and chopped

salt and **pepper**

broiled corn and avocado salsa

This salsa is delicious with grilled or roasted meats and fish. If it is kept longer than a few hours the avocado will discolor and lose its vibrancy, so make it only far enough ahead to allow the flavors to mingle and develop. Alternatively, prepare the salsa in advance without the avocado, adding it about 30 minutes before serving.

1 Plunge the corn cobs into a saucepan of boiling water, return to a boil and blanch for 3–4 minutes. Drain, rub with a little of the olive oil, and place under a preheated broiler for 10–15 minutes, turning occasionally, until tender and well toasted. Leave to cool slightly, then scrape the kernels into a bowl and set aside to cool.

2 Add the onion to the corn with the lime juice, jalapeño sauce, chili, red bell pepper, tomato, coriander, cilantro, the remaining oil, and salt and pepper. Toss gently to combine, then fold in the avocado. Taste and adjust the seasoning as necessary. Cover and chill for at least 30 minutes for the flavors to develop.

Makes 2 cups

Preparation time: 15 minutes, plus cooling and chilling time

Cooking time: 15–20 minutes

hot papaya and roasted pepper salsa

Sweet and tangy, this salsa is delicious with grilled or sautéed meat, chicken, fish, and vegetables. It is best eaten the day it is made.

1 Combine the lime juice, olive oil, and balsamic vinegar in a bowl. Add the papaya, chili, scallions, and roasted red bell peppers and toss gently until combined. Season with salt and pepper and stir in the cilantro. Cover and chill for about 30 minutes before serving to allow the flavors to blend and develop.

Makes 1³/₄ cups

Preparation time: 10–15 minutes, plus chilling time

juice of 1–2 **limes**

¹/₂ cup **light olive oil**

¹/₄ teaspoon **balsamic vinegar**

2 ripe **papayas**, peeled, seeded, and cut into ¹/₂-inch dice

¹/₂ small **red chili**, finely chopped

2 **scallions**, finely chopped

2 **roasted red bell peppers**, cored, seeded, and cut into ¹/₄-inch dice

2 tablespoons finely chopped **cilantro**

salt and **pepper**

1 **papaya**, peeled, seeded, and finely chopped

juice and finely grated zest of 1 **lime**

15-ounce can **cannellini beans**, drained

3 tablespoons chopped **cilantro**

2 **tomatoes**, chopped

1 small **green chili**, seeded and chopped

salt and **pepper**

papaya, green chili and cannellini bean salsa

1 Mix the chopped papaya with the lime juice and the grated lime zest. Season to taste with salt and pepper and stir in the cannellini beans, the cilantro, tomatoes, and the chopped green chili. Mix well and chill until ready to serve. Serve with roast loin of pork.

Makes 1³/₄ cups

Preparation time: 10 minutes, plus chilling time

mango and cucumber salsa with chili

This salsa is quick and easy to make, and can be as fiery or as refreshing as you wish—just adjust the amount of chilies or leave them out altogether. It is excellent with roasted, sautéed or grilled foods, particularly herrings and salmon, but is also perfect with cold cuts, such as salami, bresàola, or Parma ham. It will keep for several days in the refrigerator.

1 Cut the cucumber into $1/8-1/4$-inch dice and leave in a sieve to drain. Slice along each side of the flat central pit of the mango. Discard the pit and cut each piece of mango flesh into long strips $1/8-1/4$-inch thick. Remove the skin by slipping the knife between the flesh and skin and running it along its length. Chop into dice. Combine the cucumber and mango in a bowl.

2 Put the onion in a small bowl, cover with boiling water and soak for a few minutes. Drain and refresh under cold water, then pat dry with paper towels (this helps soften the flavor of the onion).

3 Add the onion to the cucumber and mango with the rest of the ingredients. Stir gently to combine. Cover and chill for a few hours to allow the flavors to mingle and develop. Serve chilled, garnished with chopped flat leaf parsley.

Makes 2$1/2$ cups

Preparation time: 10–15 minutes, plus chilling time

$1/2$ **cucumber**, peeled

1 large **mango**, ripe but still firm

$1/4$ cup finely chopped **red onion**

1 small **green chili**, seeded and finely chopped

2 tablespoons finely chopped **flat leaf parsley**

juice of 1$1/2$ **limes**

salt and **pepper**

chopped **flat leaf parsley**, to garnish

ingredients

2 tablespoons **olive oil**

1-inch piece of **fresh ginger**, peeled and finely chopped

$1/2$ teaspoon **mild curry powder**

1 small **red onion**, finely chopped

1 teaspoon **black mustard seeds**

2 **peaches**, peeled, halved, pitted and cut into small cubes

juice of 1 **lemon**

3 tablespoons roughly chopped **cilantro leaves**

salt and **pepper**

peach and ginger salsa

Mini poppadoms are ideal with this salsa.

1 Heat the olive oil in a frying pan. Add the ginger, curry powder, red onion and mustard seeds and cook gently for 3–4 minutes until the aromas are released.

2 Remove the pan from the heat and add the peaches and lemon juice. Season generously with salt and pepper, then cover and leave to rest for 30 minutes at room temperature. Transfer the salsa to a serving bowl, stir in the cilantro leaves and serve immediately.

Makes 2 cups

Preparation time: 10 minutes, plus resting time

Cooking time: 3–4 minutes

5 ounces **strawberries**, hulled and roughly chopped

$^1/_2$ ripe **mango,** peeled, pitted, and roughly chopped

$^1/_2$ ripe **papaya**, peeled, seeded, and roughly chopped

1 **orange**, segmented and roughly chopped

3 tablespoons **balsamic vinegar**

2 tablespoons **vodka**

3 tablespoons chopped **mint,** to decorate

summer fruit salsa

1 Put the strawberries, mango, papaya, and orange in a bowl and sprinkle with the balsamic vinegar and vodka. Cover and leave to infuse for at least 30 minutes before serving, decorated with a little chopped mint.

Makes 2 cups

Preparation time: 10 minutes, plus resting time

FOOD FACT

Balsamic vinegar is generally accepted to be the finest vinegar of all. A rich, sweet vinegar, it is produced in the Emilia-Romagna region of northern Italy from grape juice and aged in wooden casks for up to 50 years or more. Truly authentic, aged balsamic vinegars have a very mellow flavor and are very expensive.

pineapple salsa with chili, orange and mint

1 Put the slices of pineapple in a lightly oiled baking pan, sprinkle with the brown sugar, cumin and coriander and cook under a preheated broiler for 5 minutes, turning once halfway through cooking. Remove from the heat and allow to cool slightly.

2 Finely chop the pineapple, place it in a bowl and mix with the sun-dried chilies, orange zest and juice, mint, and vinegar. Season with salt and pepper. Cover and leave to rest for 30 minutes before serving.

Makes 2 cups

Preparation time: 10 minutes, plus resting time

Cooking time: 5 minutes

1 small **pineapple**, peeled and cut into 1-inch slices

2 tablespoons **brown sugar**

1 teaspoon ground **cumin**

1 teaspoon ground **coriander**

2 large **red sun-dried chilies**, finely chopped

grated zest and juice of 1 **orange**

$^1/_4$ cup chopped **mint**

3 tablespoons **red wine vinegar**

salt and **pepper**

2 large ripe **avocados**, halved, pitted and peeled

juice of 1 **lime** or **lemon**

1 **garlic clove**, crushed

2 tablespoons finely chopped **onion**

1 large **tomato**, skinned, seeded, and finely chopped

1–2 fresh **green chilies**, seeded and finely chopped

2 tablespoons finely chopped **cilantro leaves**

pinch of **sugar**

salt and **pepper**

cilantro sprigs, to garnish

guacamole

This thick creamy avocado purée from Mexico can be used as a dip for Crudités (see page 63), fresh Tortilla Chips (see page 52), or Pita Chips (see page 56), or eaten Mexican-style with tortillas. It can also be used as a sauce for fish and chicken. Don't purée the avocado flesh in a food processor or blender as this produces too smooth a texture.

1 Put the avocado flesh in a bowl with the lime or lemon juice and mash with a fork to make a chunky paste. Stir in the garlic, onion, tomato, chilies, cilantro, and sugar. Season with salt and pepper and add some extra lime or lemon juice, if required. Spoon the mixture into a serving bowl and garnish with cilantro sprigs. Cover with plastic wrap to help prevent discoloration and chill until required.

Makes about 2 cups

Preparation time: 10 minutes, plus chilling time

1/4 cup **green le Puy lentils**

2–3 tablespoons **green peppercorns in brine**, drained

3 tablespoons **Dijon mustard**

1/2 cup **sunflower oil**

2 tablespoons **lemon juice**

2 tablespoons **warm water**

lentil, green peppercorn and mustard dip

Serve this dip with crisp vegetables or sautéed or grilled fish. It also goes well with Crudités (see page 63). It will keep in the refrigerator for several days.

1 Bring a large saucepan of water to a boil, add the lentils and return to a boil. Cook for 10–15 minutes until just tender and beginning to turn mushy. Drain and refresh under cold water until it is completely cold.

2 Crush the peppercorns until roughly broken using a pestle and mortar. Transfer to a bowl, stir in the mustard and gradually beat in the oil, adding a little at a time. Stir in the lemon juice, warm water, and cooked lentils. Pile into a serving bowl, cover with plastic wrap and chill for at least 30 minutes.

Makes 2/3 cup

Preparation time: 10 minutes, plus cooling and chilling time

Cooking time: 10–15 minutes

baba ganoush

This Turkish spiced eggplant pâté comes in many guises, with each recipe varying slightly. Some include tahini, others yogurt; this version with its slightly unusual addition of chopped mint is particularly delicious.

1 Prick the eggplants all over with a fork and cook them in a preheated oven at 400°F for 20–30 minutes, until the skins wrinkle and the flesh feels collapsed, turning them halfway through cooking. Set aside to cool.

2 Squeeze the eggplants to release the moisture, then slice them open and scrape the flesh into a food processor. Add the garlic, cumin, tahini, mint, and tomato and process to form a fairly smooth paste, then gradually blend in the oil to soften the texture. Season with salt and pepper to taste and serve with grilled bread or pita chips.

Makes about 1¹/₄ cups

Preparation time: 10–15 minutes

Cooking time: 20–30 minutes

2 **eggplants**

1 **garlic clove**, crushed

¹/₂ teaspoon **ground cumin**

2 tablespoons **tahini**

3 tablespoons **chopped mint**

1 **tomato**, skinned, seeded, and chopped

¹/₂–²/₃ cup **extra virgin olive oil**

salt and **pepper**

Grilled Bread (see page 57) or **Pita Chips** (see page 56), to serve

chili bean dip

This spicy dip is excellent with Crudités (see page 63), corn chips or Pita Chips (see page 56). It is also good spread on bruschetta and crostini, like a pâté.

1 Halve the peppers lengthwise and scrape out the seeds. Lightly brush the bell peppers inside and out with a little oil. Place on a lightly oiled baking sheet and roast in a preheated oven at 475°F for 15 minutes. Remove the bell peppers from the oven and leave until cool enough to handle, then peel off the skins.

2 Process the bell pepper flesh, garlic, and chili in a food processor or blender until well chopped. Add the beans and paprika and continue to process until a coarse purée forms. This will only take a few seconds. Season with Tabasco™, if using, and salt and pepper. With the motor running, slowly add the remaining oil to make a thick paste.

3 Place the bean purée into a bowl and sprinkle with the chopped chives. Cover and chill until required.

Makes about 1³/₄ cups

Preparation time: 15 minutes, plus cooling and chilling time

Cooking time: 15 minutes

2 large **red bell peppers**

3 tablespoons **olive oil**

2 **garlic cloves**, crushed

1 small **red chili**, seeded and finely chopped

15-ounce can **red kidney beans**, drained

$^1/_2$ teaspoon **paprika**

few drops of **Tabasco™ sauce** (optional)

salt and **pepper**

3 tablespoons snipped **chives**, to garnish

15-ounce can **chickpeas**

2 **garlic cloves**, crushed

3–5 tablespoons **lemon juice**

$^2/_3$ cup **tahini**

$^2/_3$ cup **olive** or **sunflower oil**

$^1/_4$–$^1/_2$ cup **plain yogurt** or **hot water**

salt and **pepper**

cayenne pepper or **paprika**, to serve

hummus

1 Drain and rinse the chickpeas then put them in a food processor or blender with the garlic, lemon juice, tahini and salt and pepper to taste. Process to a smooth paste.

2 Very gradually add the oil as if making mayonnaise (see below). Stir in the yogurt or hot water to give the required consistency. Adjust the seasoning to taste.

3 Spoon the hummus into a serving dish and smooth with the back of a spoon. Pour over a little oil and dust with a sprinkling of cayenne or paprika.

Makes 1$^1/_4$–1$^1/_2$ cups

Preparation time: 10 minutes

2–8 **garlic cloves**, according to taste

$^1/_2$ teaspoon **sea salt**

2 **egg yolks***

2 tablespoons **lemon juice**

1 teaspoon **Dijon mustard**

1$^1/_4$ cups French **extra virgin olive oil**

1–2 teaspoons **boiling water** (optional)

aïoli, allioli or garlic mayonnaise

1 Crush the garlic cloves with the sea salt in a mortar or by pounding them together on a board with the side of a knife blade. Transfer to a food processor with the egg yolks, lemon juice, and mustard and process until smooth and creamy.

2 With the motor running, add the oil in a steady stream through the feeder tube until the sauce is emulsified, thick and glossy. You may need to thin it slightly by whisking in a spoonful or two of boiling water. Cover the surface with plastic wrap and chill until required.

Makes about 1$^1/_4$ cups

Preparation time: 10 minutes, plus chilling time

* Please see the FDA egg safety warning on page 4.

tapenade

The word tapenade comes from "tapeno," the old Provençal word for caper, traditionally an important ingredient. Nowadays capers are used less frequently and sometimes they are left out altogether. Tapenade will keep in a tightly covered jar in the refrigerator for several weeks.

1 Pound the olives, capers, anchovies, garlic, and mustard in a mortar to make a paste. Transfer them to a bowl and work in the oil a drop at a time initially, then add it a little more quickly. Mix in the thyme, lemon juice, and plenty of black pepper. Adjust the consistency (it should be a thick, spreadable paste) and pungency if necessary, adding more oil to mellow it. Serve at room temperature.

Makes 1²/₃ cups

Preparation time: 10 minutes

7 ounces Noyons **black olives**, pitted

2 ounces **capers**

4 **anchovy fillets**, rinsed if necessary

1–2 **garlic cloves**, crushed

2 tablespoons **Dijon mustard**

¹/₂ cup **olive oil**

1 teaspoon crumbled **thyme**

lemon juice, to taste

pepper

3 1/2 ounces **Danish blue cheese** or another **strong, creamy blue cheese**

7 ounces **cream cheese**

1/4 cup **milk**

1/3 cup chopped **chives**, plus extra for garnish

1/2 cup **shelled walnuts**, chopped, plus extra for garnish

blue cheese and walnut dip

1 Put the Danish blue and the cream cheese in a bowl with the milk and beat until smooth. Fold in the chives and walnuts. Transfer to a serving bowl and serve garnished with a few chopped walnuts and some chives.

Makes 1 3/4 cups

Preparation time: 10 minutes

FOOD FACT
Blue cheeses are curd cheeses that have bacteria injected into them so that they develop blue or green veining. Although the best blue cheeses are intensely individual, they share a sharp flavor and a crumbly texture that makes them very useful in cooking.

8 ounces deli-marinated **artichoke hearts**

3 tablespoons **olive oil**

2 teaspoons **coarse grain mustard**

2 teaspoons **clear honey**

$^1/_4$ cup **Parmesan cheese**, finely grated

$^2/_3$ cup **sour cream**

salt and **pepper**

creamy artichoke dip with mustard and parmesan

1 Put the artichoke hearts in a food processor or blender with the olive oil, mustard, honey, and Parmesan, and blend until you have a fairly smooth paste.

2 Transfer the dip to a serving bowl, season with salt and pepper and fold in the sour cream. Serve immediately.

Makes 1$^3/_4$ cups

Preparation time: 10 minutes

TIP
Artichoke hearts are sold in cans and jars. They are excellent in salads and can be sautéed in butter and sprinkled with parsley or chervil and served as a vegetable dish. They can also be tossed with pasta and Parmesan cheese to make a quick supper.

1 cup **basil leaves**

1 **garlic clove**, crushed

$^1/_3$ cup **pine nuts**

$^1/_4$ teaspoon **sea salt**

$^1/_2$–$^3/_4$ cup **extra virgin olive oil**

3 tablespoons grated **Parmesan cheese**

pepper

$^2/_3$ cup **crème fraîche**

basil leaves, to serve

pesto and crème fraîche dip

1 First make the pesto. Put the basil, garlic, pine nuts, and salt in a food processor and blend into a smooth paste. Slowly add the oil until the texture is soft but not too runny, then add the Parmesan and pepper to taste, and mix. Transfer to a bowl and cover with plastic wrap. Pesto can be kept for up to 3 days in the refrigerator.

2 To make the dip, put the crème fraîche in a bowl and lightly mix in $^1/_4$ cup of the pesto, so that the crème fraîche is streaked with the pesto. Serve scattered with basil leaves.

Makes $^3/_4$ cup

Preparation time: 10 minutes

1 cup **plain yogurt**

3-inch piece of **cucumber**, peeled and coarsely grated or chopped

3 tablespoons **chopped mint**

pinch of **ground cumin**

squeeze of **lemon** or **lime juice**

pepper

mint sprigs, to garnish

cucumber and mint raita

A mild-flavored and refreshing Indian yogurt dish, this is the perfect accompaniment to any spicy, highly seasoned meat, fish, or vegetable. A little chopped fresh chili or cilantro leaves or some mint sauce can also be added.

1 Put the yogurt in a bowl and beat lightly with a fork or whisk until smooth. Add the cucumber, mint, cumin, lemon or lime juice, and pepper and stir to combine. Cover and refrigerate until needed. Serve chilled, garnished with mint sprigs.

Makes $1^1/_4$ cups

Preparation time: 10 minutes, plus chilling time

herbed yogurt dip

1 Put the basil, parsley, lemon thyme, garlic, almonds, lemon zest, and olive oil in a small food processor or blender and blend to a fine paste. Season with salt and pepper.

2 Put the yogurt in a serving bowl and fold through the herb mixture, creating a marbled effect. Serve immediately.

Makes 1¹/₂ cups

Preparation time: 10 minutes

TIP
Greek yogurt, which is thick and creamy, makes an excellent base for a quick dip. Mix chopped or grated cucumber, chopped mint, and garlic with yogurt to make tzatziki; blend roasted and seeded yellow peppers in a food processor with soy sauce, chopped cilantro, yogurt, and a little pepper for a piquant and vivid appetizer, or, if you're really pressed for time, simply stir in some curry powder or paste.

¹/₃ cup **basil** leaves

¹/₄ cup **flat leaf parsley**

¹/₄ cup **lemon thyme**

1 **garlic clove**, peeled

¹/₄ cup **toasted almonds**

grated **zest of 1 lemon**

²/₃ cup **olive oil**

1¹/₄ cups **Greek or plain yogurt**

salt and **pepper**

3 tablespoons **olive oil**

1 small **onion**, chopped

1 **garlic clove**, crushed

$1/4$ cups **crème fraîche**

1 ounce **dried onion
soup mix**

$1/3$ cup chopped **parsley**, plus
a little extra for garnish

3 tablespoons **milk**

classic french onion dip

**This dip is very good served with thin slices of French bread, sprinkled
with a little Parmesan cheese and toasted.**

1 Heat the olive oil in a frying pan.
Add the onion and cook over a
moderate heat for 5 minutes, then
add the garlic and continue to
cook for 2 minutes until just
starting to color. Remove from the
heat and allow to cool.

2 Combine the onion mixture with
the crème fraîche, onion soup mix,
parsley, and milk. Transfer to a
serving dish and leave to rest
in the refrigerator for 1 hour to
set. Stir well and serve, garnished
with parsley.

Makes 1³/₄ cups

*Preparation time: 10 minutes,
plus cooling and chilling time*

Cooking time: 7 minutes

crab dip with horseradish

1 Put the egg yolks, vinegar, mustard, and horseradish in a food processor or blender, season with salt and pepper and blend until pale and creamy. With the motor running, gradually pour in all the oil. The mixture should be thick and glossy.

2 Transfer the mayonnaise to a bowl, stir in the crab and scallions and serve immediately.

Makes 1¹/₄ cups

Preparation time: 15 minutes

2 **egg yolks**＊

2 teaspoons **red wine vinegar**

1 teaspoon **Dijon mustard**

2 tablespoons **creamed horseradish**

²/₃ cup **olive oil**

5 ³/₄-ounce can **white crab meat,** drained

3 **scallions**, chopped

salt and **pepper**

＊ Please see the FDA egg safety warning on page 4.

indonesian peanut dipping sauce

This recipe was inspired by satay sauce, the rich, spicy, nutty Indonesian concoction made from peanuts, peanut butter, ginger, and chili. In this recipe the sauce is thicker and richer than usual, so that it can be used as a dip. It is delicious with any type of vegetable brochette or kabob, with chunky pieces of grilled vegetables and grilled skewered meats, particularly chicken.

1 Heat the oil in a saucepan and sauté the onion, garlic, ginger, and ground peanuts for 10 minutes to develop the flavors. Add the chili powder, soy sauce, peanut butter, sugar, lime juice, and coconut cream, stirring well to combine. Bring to a boil, then reduce the heat and cook gently for a further 10 minutes.

2 Transfer the sauce to a bowl and allow to cool, then cover and chill for at least 30 minutes.

Makes about 1 cup

Preparation time: 10 minutes, plus cooling and chilling time

Cooking time: 20–25 minutes

3 tablespoons **sunflower oil**

1 small **onion**, finely grated

2 **garlic cloves**, crushed

1-inch piece of **fresh ginger**, peeled and grated

$^1/_2$ cup **dry roasted peanuts**, ground in a blender or nut mill

large pinch of **hot chili powder**

$^1/_2$ teaspoon **soy sauce**

$^1/_4$ cup **crunchy peanut butter**

2–4 tablespoons **brown sugar**

3 tablespoons **lime juice**

1 cup **coconut cream**

15 medium **chilies**

1 cup **granulated sugar**

$^2/_3$ cup **rice wine vinegar**

$^2/_3$ cup **water**

$^1/_2$ teaspoon **salt**

$^1/_4$ teaspoon **pepper**

juice of 1 **lemon**

sweet chili sauce

This Thai sauce is particularly good with Thai fish cakes and deep-fried chicken or fish. It will keep for up to 1 month in the refrigerator.

1 Wearing a pair of plastic gloves, remove the seeds from the chilies and finely chop the flesh. Place the chilies in a saucepan with the sugar, rice vinegar, and water. Heat gently to dissolve the sugar then increase the heat and simmer briskly for 20–25 minutes or until the liquid has reduced to a syrup.

2 Remove the pan from the heat and leave to cool. Add the salt, pepper, and lemon juice. Pour the sauce into a container and store in the refrigerator until required.

Makes 1$^1/_4$ cups

Preparation time: 15 minutes, plus cooling time

Cooking time: 20–25 minutes

szechuan dipping sauce

A hot peppery dipping sauce, which takes its name from the fiery style of cooking of the Szechuan province of China. Although hot, it is also slightly sweet and spicy. Serve with Crudités (see page 63) or grilled vegetables. This sauce will keep for several weeks in the refrigerator without the scallions and cilantro.

1 In a screw-top jar, combine the soy sauce, sesame oil, lime juice, vinegar, chili sauce, honey, garlic, sesame seeds, and ginger. Shake well to mix. Chill in the refrigerator for a few hours so that the flavors can mingle and develop.

2 Just before serving, stir in the scallions and cilantro.

Makes ⅓ cup

Preparation time: 10 minutes, plus chilling time

¹/₃ cup **soy sauce**

3 tablespoons **light sesame oil**

3 tablespoons **lime juice**

2 tablespoons **rice wine vinegar**

2 tablespoons **sweet chili sauce**

2 tablespoons **clear honey**

2 **garlic cloves**, finely chopped

1 teaspoon **toasted sesame seeds**

1-inch piece of **fresh ginger**, peeled and finely grated

2 large **scallions**, finely chopped

2 tablespoons finely **chopped cilantro**

6 sheets **phyllo pastry**, 12 $^1/_2$ x 8 $^1/_2$ inches, defrosted if frozen

$^1/_3$ cup **butter**, melted

1 $^1/_2$ cups **Emmenthal cheese**, finely grated

phyllo and emmenthal wafers

These crisp savory wafers are composed of gossamer thin sheets of filo pastry layered with butter and finely grated Emmenthal cheese. They make excellent crackers to serve with drinks and dips, and can be stored in an airtight container for 3–4 days.

1 Lightly brush 1 sheet of phyllo pastry with butter and scatter with a little of the cheese. Put a second sheet on top, brush with melted butter and scatter with more cheese. Repeat with a third sheet, finishing with the cheese. Do the same with the remaining 3 sheets of phyllo pastry so that you have 2 stacks of pastry. Using a 3-inch plain round pastry cutter, cut the phyllo layers into circles and place them on a heavy baking sheet. Alternatively, cut the pastry into rectangular 4 x 1 $^1/_4$ inch wafers.

2 Bake the wafers in a preheated oven at 350°F for 15 minutes until crisp and light brown. Remove from the baking sheet and cool on a wire rack.

Makes 22 round crackers or 42 rectangular ones

Preparation time: 10 minutes

Cooking time: 15 minutes

1 cup **all-purpose flour**

$^1/_3$ cup **unsalted butter**, cut into small pieces

2 tablespoons **English mustard powder**

pinch of **cayenne pepper**

pinch of **salt**

1 cup **sharp Cheddar cheese**, finely grated

3–4 tablespoons **Parmesan cheese**, finely grated

3 tablespoons **black mustard seeds**

2 tablespoons **poppy seeds**

seeded cheese sablés

Serve these crisp savory crackers with dips, soup, raw vegetable salads like Crudités (see page 63), and roasted or grilled vegetables. They are perfect with cheese and chutney too, and also good as a cocktail cracker. They can be cut into any shape, served hot or cold, and they freeze well.

1 Work the flour, butter, mustard, cayenne, and salt in a food processor until the mixture resembles fine breadcrumbs. Add the Cheddar and continue to process for a few seconds until the mixture begins to come together to make a soft dough. Turn out onto a lightly floured surface and knead gently. Wrap in plastic wrap and refrigerate for about 30 minutes.

2 Roll out the pastry on a lightly floured surface to about $^1/_8$-inch thick. Cut into circles with a $2^1/_2$-inch fluted pastry cutter. Knead the trimmings together, roll out and cut out more circles.

3 Line 2 heavy baking sheets with parchment paper and place the sablés on them. Sprinkle with Parmesan and dust with mustard and poppy seeds. Bake in a preheated oven at 400°F for 9–12 minutes until crisp and light golden. Transfer to a wire rack with an offset spatula. Serve hot, or set aside to cool and store in an airtight container to serve later.

Makes about 30

Preparation time: 20 minutes, plus chilling time

Cooking time: 9–12 minutes

cheesy crisps

1 cup **sharp farmhouse** or **vegetarian Cheddar, Gruyère,** or **raclette cheese**, coarsely grated or diced

These can be served as a savory bite with drinks, or as an accompaniment with salsas and dips of your choice. The cheese can be mixed with ¼ cup chopped walnuts, pecans or hazelnuts, and seasoned with fresh thyme, ground black pepper, a little paprika, or cayenne pepper. When cold, the crisps can be stored in an airtight container for about 1 week or frozen for several weeks. If they soften, return them to a hot oven to crisp up.

1 Line several baking sheets with parchment paper. Place 2 mounds of cheese on each sheet, no more than 3½ inches in diameter and at least 4 inches apart. As it cooks, the cheese will spread and form rough circles.

2 Bake the crisps in a preheated oven at 425°F for 10 minutes until the cheese bubbles and begins to turn a very pale cream color. If they are too golden in color, they will taste bitter.

3 Allow the crisps to cool slightly, then transfer them with a spatula to a wire rack to cool completely. Serve or store as required.

Makes 8–10

Preparation time: 10 minutes

Cooking time: 10 minutes per batch

4 small **flour tortillas**

2 tablespoons **olive oil**

tortilla chips

1 Cut each tortilla into 8 triangles, place on a baking sheet and brush with a little oil. Bake in a preheated oven at 400°F for 10–12 minutes until golden and crisp. Allow to cool.

Makes 32

Preparation time: 5 minutes

Cooking time: 10–12 minutes

TIP
For extra flavor and color, add a little paprika and salt to the olive oil before brushing the tortillas with it.

Starter dough

1 cup **warm water**

$^1/_4$ teaspoon **dry active yeast**

3 cups **white bread flour**

$^1/_2$ teaspoon **sugar**

Bread dough

$1^1/_2$ teaspoons **dry active yeast**

$3^1/_2$ cups **warm water**

1 teaspoon **sugar**

6 cups **white bread flour**

2 cups **semolina**, plus extra for sprinkling

$1^1/_2$ tablespoons **salt**

sourdough bread

1 Four days before making the bread, prepare the starter dough. Pour the warm water into a small bowl and stir in the yeast to dissolve it. Add about $^1/_2$ cup of the flour and the sugar and leave to froth in a warm place for 10 minutes. Work the mixture into the remaining flour, cover with plastic wrap and leave in a warm place for at least 3 days.

2 To begin the bread dough, dissolve the yeast in $^2/_3$ cup of the warm water, add the sugar and $^1/_2$ cup of the flour and leave to froth for 10 minutes. Transfer to a large bowl and gradually work in $^1/_2$ cup of the starter dough (refrigerate the rest and use as needed), the remaining warm water and flour, the semolina, and salt until a sticky, slightly lumpy dough forms.

3 Transfer the dough to an oiled bowl, cover with oiled plastic wrap and leave in a warm place for several hours to double in size.

4 Carefully turn out the dough onto a floured surface, cut off about $^1/_2$ cup and add it to the starter dough mixture. Cut the remaining dough in half and shape each piece into a flat round. Roll the dough up, turn it 180° and repeat the rolling. Transfer to a well-floured baking sheet, sprinkle the surface with semolina and cover with a clean dish towel.

5 Leave the dough to rise for 1–2 hours, until doubled in size. Score the surface with a sharp knife and bake in a preheated oven at 450°F for 30 minutes. Cool on a wire rack.

Makes 2 round loaves

Preparation time: 40 minutes, plus resting and rising time

Cooking time: 30 minutes

6 white **pita breads**

3 **garlic cloves**, crushed

2 tablespoons **dried mixed herbs**

$^3/_4$ cup **olive oil**

2 teaspoons **mild chili powder**

2 teaspoons **paprika**

pita chips

1 Split open the pitas and then cut each half into quarters. Divide them equally between 2 large roasting pans. In the first pan rub the garlic, mixed herbs, and half the olive oil into the bread. Rub the chili powder, paprika, and the remaining oil into the second batch of bread.

2 Bake in a preheated oven at 400°F for 15 minutes or until lightly golden in color and crisp. Serve warm or cold with a selection of dips.

Makes 48

Preparation time: 10 minutes

Cooking time: 15 minutes

grilled bread

1 Sift the flours and salt into the bowl of a mixer. Stir in the yeast and then, with the dough hook turning, gradually add the water and oil to form a soft dough. Knead for 8–10 minutes, until smooth and elastic.

2 Transfer the dough to an oiled bowl, cover with a dish towel and leave to rise in a warm place for 1 hour, until doubled in size.

3 Divide the dough into eight pieces and roll out each one on a lightly floured surface to form an oval about 8 inches long, brush with a little oil and leave to rise for about 10 minutes.

4 Heat a grillpan or heavy-based pan until really hot and cook the bread for about 2 minutes on each side, until spotted with brown and puffed up. Serve immediately.

Makes 8

Preparation time: 15 minutes, plus rising time

Cooking time: 4 minutes per batch

4 cups **all-purpose flour**

2 cups **wholewheat flour**

2 teaspoons **salt**

1 teaspoon **fast-acting yeast**

2 cups **warm water**

2 tablespoons **extra virgin olive oil**, plus extra for brushing

4 large **baking potatoes**

$1/2–3/4$ cup **olive oil**

$1/2$ teaspoon **salt**

1–2 teaspoons **chili powder**, to taste

spicy oven fries

Use as little or as much chili powder as you like to coat these oven-roasted potato wedges.

1 Cut each potato lengthwise into 8 wedges and place in a large bowl. Add the oil, salt, and chili powder and toss until evenly coated.

2 Transfer the potatoes to a baking sheet and roast in a preheated oven at 425°F for 15 minutes. Turn them over and cook for a further 15 minutes. Turn once more and cook for a final 25–30 minutes until crisp and golden.

3 Allow to cool slightly and serve with a spicy dip.

Makes 32

Preparation time: 5 minutes

Cooking time: about 1 hour

chicken skewers with fruit and nut couscous

1 Cut the chicken into long thin strips, place them in a shallow dish and add the olive oil, garlic, spices, and lemon juice. Stir well, then cover and leave to marinate for 2 hours. Thread the chicken strips onto 8 small, presoaked wooden skewers.

2 Broil or grill the chicken skewers for 4–5 minutes on each side, until charred and cooked through. Serve with the fruit and nut couscous, garnished with pomegranate seeds, lemon wedges, and cilantro sprigs, and a selection of dips.

Serves 4

Preparation time: 20–30 minutes, plus marinating time

Cooking time: 8–10 minutes, plus couscous

FRUIT AND NUT COUSCOUS

Pour $2^1/_2$ cups stock over $^3/_4$ cup couscous and steam for 8–10 minutes. Meanwhile, sauté 1 small onion, 1 crushed garlic clove, and 1 teaspoon each ground cinnamon, cumin, pepper, and ginger in 3 tablespoons olive oil. Mix in 1 cup chopped dried fruit and $^1/_2$ cup chopped, toasted blanched almonds and remove from the heat. Stir the fruit and nut mixture into the couscous with 3 tablespoons oil, 2 tablespoons lemon juice, and 3 tablespoons chopped cilantro and season to taste.

1 pound skinless **chicken breast fillets**

3 tablespoons **extra virgin olive oil**

2 **garlic cloves**, crushed

$^1/_2$ teaspoon each **ground cumin, turmeric,** and **paprika**

2 teaspoons **lemon juice**

dips, to serve

To garnish
seeds from $^1/_2$ **pomegranate**

lemon wedges

cilantro sprigs

1 pound **beef rump steak,** cut lengthwise into thin strips

Marinade

$^1/_2$ cup **coconut milk**

3 tablespoons **soy sauce**

1 **red chili**, finely chopped

2 **garlic cloves**, crushed

grated zest and juice of 1 **lime**

To serve

crisp **green salad leaves**

Indonesian Peanut Dipping Sauce (see page 45)

lime wedges

beef satay

1 Put all the marinade ingredients in a bowl and mix together. Add the beef slices and mix well. Cover and leave to marinate in the refrigerator for at least 4 hours. Soak 8 bamboo skewers in water for at least 30 minutes.

2 Drain the beef, keeping the marinade to one side, then thread the beef in a zig-zag pattern onto the prepared skewers. Put the skewers into a lightly oiled roasting pan and cook under a preheated broiler for 7–8 minutes, turning them and spooning a little of the marinade over them from time to time while they are cooking. Serve the beef strips on crisp green salad leaves with some peanut sauce and garnish with lime wedges.

Serves 4

Preparation time: 15 minutes

Cooking time: 7–8 minutes

1½ pounds **assorted vegetables**, such as bell peppers, zucchini, eggplant, onions, French beans, cauliflower, mushrooms, chopped

sunflower oil, for frying

fresh herbs or **salad leaves**, to garnish

Aïoli (see page 34), to serve

Batter
1 large **egg**

1 cup **beer**, very well chilled

1 cup **all-purpose flour**

½ teaspoon **baking powder**

salt and **pepper**

vegetable tempura

1 About 20 minutes before cooking, prepare the batter. With a small wire whisk, beat the egg well in a large bowl, Still beating, add the beer in a thin stream. Sift the flour, baking powder, and a pinch of salt into another bowl, stir in pepper to taste and place on top of the egg and beer mix. Stir with the whisk, barely enough to mix. Do not overbeat. Cover and leave to rest for about 10 minutes.

2 Heat the oil in a deep-fryer to 375°F. Dip the vegetables in the batter, one type at a time. Fry no more than 6 pieces at once or the temperature of the oil will drop and make the batter greasy. Zucchini, onions, cauliflower, and mushrooms take 3–5 minutes; bell peppers, eggplant, and beans about 3 minutes. The batter should be puffy, crisp, and golden, the vegetables just tender.

3 Transfer the vegetables to an baking dish or tray lined with paper towels and keep warm in a preheated oven at 375°F until they are all cooked. They will hold quite successfully for about 30 minutes.

4 Arrange the fritters on a large platter around a bowl of sauce, or pile about 9 fritters in the center of individual plates and put a few spoonfuls of aïoli on the side. Garnish with herbs or salad leaves and serve immediately.

Serves 6–8

Preparation time: about 20 minutes, plus resting time

Cooking time: 3–5 minutes per batch